GIRL TALK

How to survive

DATING

Lisa Miles and Xanna Eve Chown

rosen publishing's
rosen central

NEW YORK

This edition published in 2014 by:

The Rosen Publishing Group, Inc.
29 East 21st Street, New York, NY 10010

Designer: Jeni Child
Editor: Joe Harris
Consultants: Gill Lynas and Emma Hughes
Picture research: Lisa Miles and Xanna Eve Chown
With thanks to Bethany Miller
Picture credits: All images: Shutterstock

Library of Congress Cataloging-in-Publication Data

Miles, Lisa
How to survive dating/[Lisa Miles and Xanna Eve Chown].—1st ed.—New York: Rosen, c2014
        p. cm.—(Girl talk)
Includes index.
ISBN: 978-1-4777-0705-0 (Library Binding)
ISBN: 978-1-4777-0718-0 (Paperback)
ISBN: 978-1-4777-0719-7 (6-pack)
1. Dating (social customs)—Juvenile literature. 2. Teenage girls—Juvenile literature. I. Chown, Xanna Eve. II. Title.
HQ801 .M55 2014
646.77

Manufactured in China

CPSIA Compliance Information: Batch #S13YA: For further information, contact Rosen Publishing, New York, New York, at 1-800-237-9932.

Contents

Introduction

THE TRUTH ABOUT DATING 4

Boys, boys, boys!

DIARY: STORIES FROM MY LIFE .. 6

ARE YOU READY TO DATE? 8

FRIENDS – OR MORE? 10

FLIRTING FUN 12

QUIZ: SHOULD YOU
  DATE HIM?...................................14

Taking the plunge

DIARY: STORIES FROM MY LIFE . 16

THE BIG ASK 18

FIRST DATE 20

IT'S IN HIS KISS... 22

IS IT LOVE? 24

QUIZ: FAIRY TALE OR
  MAJOR FAIL? 26

Getting serious

DIARY: STORIES FROM MY LIFE..28

BEYOND FIRST BASE 30

BEST FRIENDS – DON'T
  FORGET THEM 32

PARENT PROBLEMS 34

IT'S OVER 36

QUIZ: ARE YOU DATING
  SAVVY? 38

Girl Talk Extra

BOY TALK....................................40

HEALTHY YOU! 42

FAQS 44

GLOSSARY...................................46

  GET HELP! 47

  INDEX...........................48

THE TRUTH
about dating

Dating. Why do we do it? Well, for a start it's fun – or it's meant to be. Dating can be exciting, confusing, mysterious and even a bit scary, but it's all part of growing up. Learning how to handle relationships helps you learn about yourself.

Getting to know him

✳ Dating is the way you get to know a potential partner. By spending time together, you work out if you want to be in a relationship with him.

Healthy relationships should be based on communication, honesty, trust and respect. Sound heavy? Maybe. But if a boy doesn't respect you, why would you want to spend time with him? ("He's sooo cute!" is not good enough!)

● GIRL TO GIRL

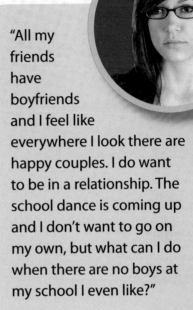

"I'm 14 but my mom doesn't think I'm ready to date. I've been asked out by boys a few times, but I always have to say no because of her. My friends say I should just not tell her, but I would feel bad. Plus if she found out I would be grounded forever!"

"All my friends have boyfriends and I feel like everywhere I look there are happy couples. I do want to be in a relationship. The school dance is coming up and I don't want to go on my own, but what can I do when there are no boys at my school I even like?"

THE LOW DOWN

The average age for a person to begin dating is 13 – but of course, there are a lot of people who start much later! It's better to decide when you want to start dating based on whether you feel ready, rather than how old you are.

"The worst date I've been on was a blind date. He kept putting his arm around me in the movie theater and I kept trying to shake it off! The best date was with my friend's brother's friend. We just went for a walk by the river – but it was SO romantic!"

Boys, boys, boys!

Stories from my life

I knew something was up when Sophie was waiting for me at the bus stop. She's always late, and I mean always. Then I noticed that she had this crazy grin all over her face... "All right," I said. "Spill."

So she did. All the way to school. And then all the way through Geography. And French. And all break time. Gavin only asked her out! And she has had a crush on him ever since he moved to our school last term. He's definitely cute – dark hair, dark eyes, nice smile – but he's not my type. He's totaly into sports, and I like guys that are more artsy. When I told Sophie she laughed and said I didn't have a type because I'd never been out with ANYONE. Ouch.

But she's right. I haven't had a boyfriend yet and loads of girls in my class have. So now I can't help thinking...

Is there something wrong with me?

Help! My friends are totally loved up!

TOP FIVE... worst things your friend might do when she has a new boyfriend

1 *Talk about how much she likes him ALL the time!*

2 *Start every sentence with "Kevin says…"*

3 *Stop hanging out with you and start spending all her time with him.*

4 *Keep trying to set you up with his (gross) best friend.*

5 *Tell him all your secrets. Gulp!*

THE LOW DOWN

Did you know?

The scientific name for kissing is osculation.

ARE YOU READY TO date?

Talking (sensibly) to your parents about dating will show them you are mature.

Some people think they should start dating because they've reached a certain age, others because all their friends are doing it. But in reality people are ready at different times – and that's fine. A date isn't going to be much fun if you are scared, or don't actually like the boy you are with!

Questions to ask yourself

* Are you comfortable with the idea of kissing someone?

* Would you be able to cope if you were dumped?

* Are your parents OK with the idea of your going on dates?

* Are you able to tell your date how far you want to take the relationship?

If you can answer yes to all of these, the chances are, you are ready! But don't worry if you are not. It's OK to take your time. Rushing into things is never a good idea.

Mom said my sister was "boy crazy." I think maybe she's just crazy!

THE LOW DOWN

Boy crazy !

When a girl is "boy crazy," it means that everything else takes second place! Having a boyfriend is more important to her than anything. She watches boys, flirts with boys and is always trying to meet and talk to them – or talk to you about them!

Some girls are boy crazy because they need a lot of attention and think this is a good way to get it. Others think that having a boyfriend will give them power, status and independence.

But in reality, it's better to have balance. Having a boyfriend shouldn't be

Never ditch your friends for a boy!

the only thing that makes you feel happy, secure and self-confident. It's great to be interested in boys. But it's also great to like yourself for who you are – and to have a good group of friends you can hang out with.

Friends – OR MORE?

You like the same music, you find the same things funny, you love to chat and you're always hanging out at his house. He's one of your best friends! Then, one day something changes and suddenly you can't help thinking... perhaps you should be dating?

When you want to date him ...

Dating a friend can be tricky – if things go wrong, you're unlikely to go back to being friends in the same way you were before. It's a risk, but if it's one you want to take, try this:

* Casually bring up the idea of being a couple. For example, you might make a joke about it.

* Then ask him in a less jokey way if he's ever thought what you would be like as a couple.

* If he laughs it off, you can still bluff your way out of it with your dignity intact.

* But if he says yes, you can say that you do too – then ask what he thinks you should do about it.

He asked her out. Her friends couldn't bear to watch.

Keeping it real:

How to say no!

What if your friend wants to date you, but you don't feel the same way. You just feel guilty, embarrassed, annoyed, confused, tongue-tied...

- ☑ Stop! It's ok to say no when someone asks you out, as long as you do it kindly and respect the fact that it has taken courage to ask.

- ☑ Try saying that you don't feel the same way, but you do want to be friends.

- ☑ Give him a hug and reassure him that there are other girls out there who'd love to date him.

GIRL TALK

Real-life advice

Trust your own feelings and if you need to let someone down be kind. Treat them in the same way you would want to be treated, and hopefully you'll stay friends.

Flirting

Some girls seem to have no trouble at all talking to boys. Others get shy and tongue-tied at the very thought. Some THINK they can talk to boys, but everyone else can see they're trying too hard!

The fine art of flirting

You want them to know you exist, but you don't want to come across as desperate. Here are some tips to remember.

Break the ice by cracking a joke, or just smiling and making eye contact – you don't need to launch into your life story.

* Pay attention to the way he reacts to you. If he steps away or makes an excuse to leave, you are trying too hard.

* Don't mumble, shuffle or look at your feet. Stand confidently and smile.

* Always leave him wanting more. If you can sense a topic of conversation is coming to an end, make an excuse, smile and leave when you're on top!

I can't believe my headphones broke. Again!

THE LOW DOWN

Body language decoded

If a boy likes you he might:

✳ Smile when he sees you

✳ Raise his eyebrows when he sees you

✳ Point his hands and feet toward you when he is sitting next to you

✳ Look at your lips when you talk

If a boy is not interested he might:

✳ Cross his arms in front of him

✳ Avoid making eye contact

✳ Keep his posture really stiff and straight when talking to you

✳ Wrinkle his nose when he talks

TALKING *Point*

Experts think that words count for only about 7 percent of what we communicate. Things like tone of voice and body language make up the rest. Do you think this is true?

13

SHOULD YOU date him?

Is he really the one for you? Answer the questions, follow the arrows and find out!

START HERE!

Do you want to talk about him all the time?
YES
NO

Have you tested out the way your names sound together?
YES
NO

Do your friends like him?
YES
NO

Have you ever dreamed about him?
YES
NO

Do you get jealous when you see him with other girls?
YES
NO

Do you feel you have a real connection?

YES

NO

Does he have a good reputation?

YES

NO

YES

Do you smile whenever you see him?

NO

YES

If you got together, would you have much to talk about?

NO

ASK HIM OUT!

It sounds like you're spending a lot of time dreaming about him. Why not see if your dreams can come true?

THINK IT THROUGH!

You like him, but there's something missing. Perhaps he's friend material – not the one.

TIME TO WAIT!

It sounds like you're just looking for a boy to be with. Maybe it's better to wait for the butterflies!

Taking the plunge

Stories from my life

So, there was me worrying that I hadn't been on a date when – Jake asked me out! He's friends with Gavin, Sophie's new boyfriend. I know him a bit, not very well, but Sophie says he's really nice, and she knows because she's been hanging out with him and Gavin a lot. I kind of wonder if she TOLD him to ask me out – otherwise it came out of the blue, right? I guess that's OK.

Anyway, he asked me to go bowling with him on Saturday night. Sophie and Gavin are going, too, so it's going to be a double date, which is good. So all I need to worry about is: what to wear, what to say, what to do, whether he will like me when he gets to know me and – OMG – whether I'll like him.

Wish me luck!

He asked me out and I said yes!

GIRL TO GIRL

"I've known this guy for a while and everyone says he is in love with me. He asked me out on a date and I said no really nicely, but now he won't talk to me. When we go out he just sits there and stares into the air like I'm not there. I feel bad, but I know it would have been worse for both of us if I'd said yes."

"There was this guy I liked for ages and I finally told him how I felt a couple of weeks ago. He said he felt the same, which was amazing, but he still hasn't asked me out. My friend says I should have made sure we arranged a date, and I guess she's right. Now I just need to get some more courage and try again!"

"This guy asked me out by text, and I said yes. But then we didn't see each other for ages. It was SO awkward when we saw each other, like neither of us knew how to act. I couldn't help being shy, even though we'd been messaging each other like crazy!"

TALKING *Point*

Do you think there's a right and a wrong way to ask someone out? What would be the best way?

THE BIG ask

You've probably spent a lot of time dreaming of this moment... when the guy you REALLY like asks you out on a date. But have you thought about what you'll say when he asks you? Will you act cool and confident or will you turn into a giggling wreck?

Here's a few dos and don'ts to keep you on track.

DON'T say you'll get back to him with an answer. He'll think you need time to look for an excuse or that you need to check with your friends.

DO smile!

DON'T say "Yes!" – you will sound desperate. Go for something more relaxed like "Yeah, sure," or "Sounds fun."

DO ask a follow up question about where you will go, but keep it casual. "Got anywhere in mind?" sounds like you're interested, and is a better bet than demanding to know about times and locations.

DO try to look calm. Shaking or giggling are signs that you are nervous, so try to keep it under control.

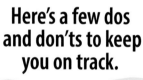

Who, me?

All about you *Should you ask him out?*

It may seem like it's more socially acceptable for a boy to ask a girl out. But when you like someone, it can be very frustrating waiting for them to make the first move. You know you'd be perfect together, so why do you have to wait…and wait… and wait? So – should you do it?

Yes
Most guys actually say they're fine with it when a girl asks them out – it takes the pressure off them! And, let's face it, this is the 21st century.

Maybe
Maybe it depends on the boy. If you know he likes you, but you also know he's very shy, you might HAVE to give him a push in the right direction, otherwise you'll never get anywhere!

No
Some guys love being the ones who do all the chasing – they think it's their role to ask girls out. They'd rather you drop a few signs that you're interested and wait for them to ask.

THE LOW DOWN   How to ask a boy out:

1. Make sure you're somewhere you can talk to him casually, and he's not with a bunch of his friends.
2. Think of a place you would like to go. "Will you come to the party/movies/bowling with me?" is better than "Let's date!"
3. Make sure you are prepared for his answer. If it's no, say "No worries, see you around…" and walk away – and have somewhere to walk to! If it's yes, smile and say "Great!" Then you can discuss details and swap numbers.

FIRST date

R emember, it's more sensible (and safer) to spend time in public places on a first date. If he really likes you, he'll be happy to go somewhere you like.

Where to go

If he asks you over to his house and his parents are out, say no. This doesn't make you boring – and it may save you from a very awkward situation. Suggest that you go somewhere else, like:

* The park
* A café
* A pizza place
* The movies
* The bowling alley
* An ice-skating rink

Winter date – good for clinging on to his hand when you wobble!

Summer date – chilling in the park all day!

Keeping it real:
First date dos and don'ts

☑ **DON'T** radically change your style. He asked you out because he liked you – not a new you in crazy heels and make-up.

☑ **DO** remember to ask him about himself, rather than hogging all the conversation.

☑ **DON'T** tell mean stories about your friends (or his!).

☑ **DO** have a few subjects of conversation up your sleeve, just in case.

☑ **DON'T** insist that he meet your family straight away.

Remember, whatever you do, try to stay relaxed and be yourself!

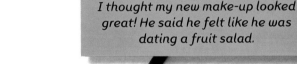

I thought my new make-up looked great! He said he felt like he was dating a fruit salad.

GiRL TALK

Real-life advice

On a first date it's good to act like yourself – and try not to be shy. Be interested in what he says so he knows you like him or he might be a bit put off. Keep calm! He's a person too.

IT'S IN his kiss...

Everyone remembers their first kiss – whether it was scary, cute, embarrassing, or hilarious. But if you want your first kiss to be more sweet than awkward, it's a good idea not to rush into things.

Kissing don'ts

* Don't have bad breath. If you've eaten onions or garlic before the kiss, try to chew gum! (But don't have it in your mouth when you kiss! Gross.)

* Don't laugh during or after the kiss. You're probably giggling because you're nervous – but he might think that you are laughing at him.

* Don't flinch or move backwards (assuming you DO want to kiss him!) – he could think you're disgusted by him!

* Don't worry if something goes wrong. You can learn from it, laugh about it and put it down to experience.

Don't do this. Ever.

Keeping it real:

Are you worried that ...

 ... you won't be able to breathe?

It's absolutely fine to take a break every 30 seconds or so for a breath. Pull away gently, keeping eye contact – and smile.

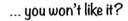 **... you won't like it?**

Lots of people don't the first time – and that's fine. Maybe you're not ready, or you just aren't with the right person. Don't spend time worrying that there's something wrong with you. Just give it some time until you think you're ready to try again.

 **... you'll bump teeth?**

Well, sometimes this happens – but it's usually due to nerves or haste. Stay calm and take it slow. If it happens, take a break, smile and try again – but not so hard!

THE LOW DOWN

Braces and glasses

If you both wear glasses, you could take them off just before you kiss to avoid clinking. If you wear braces, make sure you don't press too hard in case it hurts his lips. Don't worry – you are unlikely to get tangled up – that's just something that happens in movies.

Kissing in mid-air. Advanced level only!

IS IT love?

Being in love can feel different for everyone. However, it is easy to confuse love with lust – strong feelings based on physical attraction, or with obsession – a major crush that's taking over your mind.

How can you tell if you're in love?

You probably wouldn't have to ask if you were! There are no hard and fast rules about love, but here are some pointers.

* He makes you feel confident and positive.
* You completely trust him.
* You're not interested in other guys.
* You can relax and be yourself around him.
* You think about him all the time.

True love...

* means loving someone for who they are, not who you want them to be.
* means staying true to yourself.
* should make you feel appreciated and secure.
* is about more than just physical affection.
* is an equal partnership, and does not involve controlling behavior.

THE LOW DOWN

Could I be falling in love with a female friend?

Sometimes, it's hard to tell the difference between intense admiration and affection for a friend (she's sooo amazing!), and romantic attraction.

You could be gay (attracted to other girls) or bisexual (attracted to both boys and girls). However, knowing whether you are gay or bisexual isn't easy to work out. It's normal to sometimes be attracted to

the same sex, and it doesn't always mean you are not heterosexual (attracted to guys). Take time to work out what you want, and don't be in a rush to label yourself.

If you are looking for more advice, turn to the Get help! section on page 47.

GiRL TALK

Real-life advice

A crush is different from love. A crush is the feeling that you really like someone because they're cute. But love is about really knowing someone better than anyone else – and caring about that person during good AND bad times.

Is it love? Or does she just want a lift over that puddle?

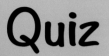

FAIRY TALE OR
major fail?

Answer the questions as honestly as you can, then give yourself a point for every time you said yes. Check your score opposite!

1. **Are you into the same kind of things, such as music or sports?**
   Yes
   No

2. **Do your friends sometimes hang out together?**
   Yes
   No

3. Do you sometimes see him when he's at home with his family?
Yes
No

4. Do you like HIS friends?
Yes
No

5. Does he like YOUR friends?
Yes
No

6. Does he take every opportunity to hold hands when you're together?
Yes
No

7. Do you love talking to him about any old stuff?
Yes
No

8. Does he make you laugh (in a good way!)?
Yes
No

9. Do you think he has a great sense of style?
Yes
No

10. Do you think he's mega-cute?
Yes
No

1-3 Fail!

Mmm... there's an attraction there, but is it good enough to last? Maybe you should find out if you have something more in common – otherwise your relationship might be fading fast...

4-7 Fizzing?

Hey, you two are a cool couple but sometimes you're in tune with each other and other times not so much. There's definitely something happening – but is it fizzing up or fizzling out?

7-8 Fate!

Wow! You're really attracted to each other but you also have loads in common. You like each other's way of doing things and that's going to help keep you together. It's fate!

Getting serious

Stories from my life

I bet you're wondering how the date went, right? Well, it was... fantastic! I was feeling really nervous when I turned up at the bowling place, but it really helped that Sophie was there! I'm not great at bowling, but it turns out neither is Jake. So we both laughed at how competitive Sophie and Gavin were being – and it really broke the ice.

After bowling we all went for a burger, which was great, too. Jake admitted that Sophie had suggested he asked me out, but he said he was REALLY glad she had. I couldn't stop smiling! And guess what?

We're going out again next week. Watch this space...

Bad bowler – great date!

GIRL TO GIRL

"I didn't feel nervous at all on our first date, or the ones that followed. But I did get nervous when he invited me home to meet his family. I knew HE liked me, but I was scared that they wouldn't. I hardly said a word the whole time, but I think it went OK!"

"After we'd been going out for a few weeks, he suddenly said 'I love you.' It was totally unexpected and I didn't know what to say. I said 'I like you, too,' then felt like a complete idiot. I think I need to talk to him properly!"

"I think I'm in love with Will but I don't think he feels the same. He seems happy whether we're together or not but I miss him like crazy when he's not around and it makes me unhappy. I'm scared in case he breaks up with me."

TALKING *Point*

How long do you think you have to know someone before you know that you really like him? Can you fall in love with someone you haven't dated?

BEYOND first base

So the first date is over and it all went brilliantly. You've been on a few more dates and you definitely like each other. You've even kissed. So what next?

It's your choice

A lot of girls and guys brag about sex and tell their friends they're doing it. But there are three things you need to know.

* What they say isn't always true.

* Not everyone is the same. Even if your friends are doing it, it doesn't mean you should.

* If your boyfriend wants to do more kissing and touching than you do, it's OK to say no.

Just because your boyfriend is a guy, it doesn't mean that he wants to be pressured by you, either.

All about you

Under pressure

Sometimes in a relationship, a person may try to persuade you to do things that you are not comfortable with. They might pressure you to have sex before you feel ready, or ask you to stop seeing certain friends, or to change your hobbies and interests.

If this ever happens to you, remember that no one is "in charge" of a relationship, and it's never OK to try to force someone to do something he or she does not want to.

It might seem hard, but the best decision is always to stand up for yourself and be true to your feelings. And if your boyfriend keeps pushing after you say no, then it's time to finish the relationship.

GIRL TALK

Real-life advice

If you think someone is trying to force you into doing anything you don't want to do, you need to tell that person how you feel. You will know when you're ready — it doesn't have to be now.

BEST FRIENDS – DON'T
forget them

You just love spending time with your boyfriend! That's great for you, but how are your friends taking it? In fact, have you seen them lately?

Don't neglect your friends!

Being part of a couple is a great feeling, especially when it's all brand-new. But it's an easy mistake to put all your focus on your boyfriend and lose touch with your girlfriends!

It's great when there are no boys... because then we can gossip about boys!

You may be wrapped up in each other, but it's never a good idea for you to stop seeing your own friends. Everyone needs to hang out with their friends from time to time and give their boyfriend or girlfriend a bit of space. You never know when you're going to need your friends – or when they might need you. And if you split with your boyfriend, the last thing you want to find out is that you have no friends.

Keeping it real:
Ways to include everyone!

There's no reason why you can't hang out with your friends and your boyfriend at the same time! Here are some suggestions of what you can do together.

☑ **Sports activities** – any team sport or activity such as bowling, tennis or biking can be fun. Split into teams for a bit of healthy competition!

☑ **Make pizza** – ask your friends over for a pizza-making party. You and your boyfriend (or best friend) could cook and the others can come along to eat.

☑ **Dinner dates** – go to a lively burger joint for dinner. Have a laugh, listen to music and share French fries!

☑ **Take a trip** – a day out to the beach or shopping in the city. You can split up into smaller groups to shop and then meet for lunch together.

☑ **Movie time** – going to the movies is always a winner. It's great for groups – but just make sure you're sitting next to your guy so you can hold his hand in the scary parts!

TALKING Point

Would you prefer a double date to a regular one? Who would you go with? Who wouldn't you go with? Why?

Parent PROBLEMS

It's not always easy to talk to your parents about dating. They might think you're not ready – or perhaps they don't like the boy you've chosen to date. So how can you prevent a big argument?

Just keep talking!

The best advice is to try to talk to your parents honestly. They're going to worry more – and be more difficult to handle – if they feel like you're excluding them and they don't know what's going on.

What to say

If you've been asked out by someone and you're planning to go on a date, just bite the bullet and tell them straight: "Mom, Leon asked me out on a date and we're going to the movies on Saturday. Is that OK with you?" Hopefully your mom or dad will understand and you can talk about the date.

If your parents want to meet your date, ask him to come around after school or over the weekend when your parents will be there.

All about you   Dating dilemma

There will always be times when you fall out with your family. But try not to let it happen too often!

If your parents hit the roof or forbid you to go on the date, it's more difficult to cope with. You might have to do some negotiating if you still want to go out with him. Whatever happens, try not to sulk or argue. It won't be helpful.

* Stay calm – if you can!

* Try to find out why they object. Maybe they will be OK with the date if you go in a group, instead of as a couple.

* Suggest that they meet the boy a few times before they're happy for you to go out with him on your own.

GIRL TALK

Real-life advice

If you're not allowed to date, you may think your parents are being mean, but they have been through all this themselves – and they are only trying to protect you.

IT'S over!

It's sad, but sometimes a relationship doesn't work out. Perhaps you know it's over – but he hasn't figured it out yet. How do you tell him? Or maybe he was the one who dumped you. How do you cope?

You're dumped!

If he says he doesn't want to go out anymore, try to accept it gracefully. You could ask for a simple reason to help you get over it, but he might be reluctant to talk too much. Find a friend and talk it over with her. Remember that no matter how bad you may feel now, things will eventually get better.

He's dumped!

If you're the one who wants to end it, you just have to be brave and tell him. There's no point in carrying on if the spark has gone, or if every time you see him he drives you nuts (in a bad way!). Don't forget, everyone has feelings, so let him down as gently as you can.

It's funny, but we don't talk anymore...

TOP FIVE... ways to break up with him nicely!

1. Always tell him yourself. Never get your friend to do it for you.

2. Tell him face-to-face if you can. It's easier that way for both of you, as at least you can have a chance to discuss it if you need to.

3. Tell him somewhere private so that he doesn't have to face his friends if he doesn't want to.

4. Just give him a simple reason why you don't want to be together – don't attack his personality, as that's not fair.

5. Keep it short – otherwise the embarrassment will be too much for both of you.

I told him that I needed more space. I'm not sure he understood – he just sat farther away!

TALKING Point

Have you ever broken up with someone? What advice would YOU give to a friend in the same situation?

ARE YOU
dating savvy?

So how much do you know about dating? Answer this true or false quiz to find out. Check your answers, give yourself a point for every one you got right, then check your results.

1. On a first date, you should always go somewhere public.
True
False

2. When kissing, it's a good idea to click teeth.
True
False

3. You should NEVER break up with someone face-to-face.
True
False

4. A first date is only a success if he kisses you.
True
False

5. On a date you should ask your date questions about himself and what he likes.
True
False

6. It's NEVER a good idea to date a friend.
True
False

7. The best advice is to always tell your parents where you're going on your date.
True
False

8. If a boy likes you he might smile a lot when he sees you.
True
False

ANSWERS

1. True
2. False
3. False
4. False
5. True
6. False
7. True
8. True

1-2 points

Maybe you need to know a few more dating rules before you go on any more dates. Don't worry, you've got lots of time to learn!

3-6 points

You're getting good at this! A few more dates and you'll be the expert on dating.

7-8 points

You're well up on the dating game. If your friends don't come to you for advice – they should!

Boy talk
FROM HIS POINT OF VIEW

When you first start dating, the chances are that going on dates are new for your boyfriend, too. Here are some important things to know about boys and dating!

Going out... the rules

✳ Despite what you might think, lots of boys are shy. It takes a lot of courage to ask a girl out. He's putting himself up for instant rejection – possibly in front of his friends and your girlfriends.

✳ If you do start going out as a steady couple, don't expect him to cut off friendships with his friends – or other girls. Don't be jealous of his other friendships. He won't like it if he feels you're being possessive.

✳ Remember – not all boys are alike. Some are emotional, some are clingy, some are independent. It's all about finding someone who suits you!

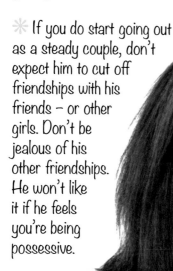

Uh-oh, he's getting emotional again.

I'm SO crazy about her, I have to tell her now!

BOYS SAY...

"I asked my friend out when we were walking home from school. She looked really awkward and muttered something about not really wanting to. I was totally embarrassed at the time but at least I tried. I'm going out with someone else now. I just put it down to experience."

"I liked this girl for ages and ages but never had the guts to ask her out. Then I found out from friends at school that she was going to ask me out! I didn't believe them – but then she did. Success!"

"I'm going out with a girl who is really cool. She doesn't get jealous if I want to go out with my friends and sometimes we all go out as a big group. I really like her because she lets me be myself."

HEALTHY you!

We all know it's important to keep your body healthy, but it's just as important to keep your emotions healthy. And if you're dating someone, your emotions are likely to be up and down, depending on how things are going.

Body and mind

If you're worried about your feelings, losing sleep or not eating properly, then you could be making yourself unwell. Here are the important things to remember about staying healthy – and happy!

* Do **some exercise** – go for a long walk, a swim or a bike ride. Exercise clears your head and makes you feel happier, as well as being good for your body!

* **Have eight or nine of hours sleep** at night – especially on a school night.

* **Eat healthily** and have regular meals – and don't skip breakfast!

* **Spend time with your best friends.** Talking things through helps and it's never a good idea to abandon your friends when you're going out with a guy.

THE LOW DOWN

Broken-hearted!

If you've just split up with someone, an emotional upheaval can lead to stress – and that's not good! Common signs of stress include:

* headaches and tension

* irritability and losing your temper

* worrying, feeling low or feeling unsociable

* difficulty in concentrating at school

* changing your eating habits

I can't think about my history project... because Ryan and I are history.

You can't change what has happened, but you can change the way that you deal with stress, which in turn can bring back feelings of happiness. Top stress-beating tips include:

* making time to relax. Have a warm bath, read, do some exercise, listen to music or do something else that makes you happy!

* talking to someone. Share your problems with a friend, parent or other adult who is responsible for you.

* avoiding stressful situations where you can. If you know that he goes to art club, for instance, avoid going there yourself for a while until you can cope better.

FAQs

Q My boyfriend wants to go past first base and I'm not sure. What do I say to him? I'm scared he'll break up with me.

A *Be honest with him – tell him that you don't feel comfortable with what he's asking you to do. If he breaks up with you over that, then he's not the right person for you and you need to move on. That might feel scary, but it's the right decision.*

Q I'm going out with a boy I've known for ages, but I think I just want to be friends. How do I get out of this?

A *Tell him you really like him as a person and want to be friends, but you don't think you're suited to being a couple. Remember to let him down as gently as you can – and tell him yourself in private, not in front of his friends. You never know, he might feel the same way. If he's upset, don't push him into meeting up as friends just yet. Just leave him alone to get over it for a while – he might come around in time.*

Q I asked a boy out and he said no. Everyone knows about it – how will I ever get over it?

A *It took a lot of courage for you to ask him out, so be proud that you were brave enough to do it. Everyone goes through rejection at some point but it doesn't mean you won't find someone else and be happy with them. Your real friends won't think less of you for trying, so give yourself a bit of time to get over it.*

Q My boyfriend dumped me. We were only going out together for a few months but I really loved him. Should I ask him if he'll go back out with me again?

A *Do you know the reason why he broke up with you? If not, try asking him – and that will give you a clue as to whether he's likely to want to give the relationship another try. But if he ended it, it's likely that he doesn't want to be with you right now, so you might have to accept that. Talk about it to your friends – they will be able to help you.*

Q I know I'm not old enough for a sexual relationship right now, but I keep worrying about what's going to happen when I'm older. How will I know what to do?

A *You'll know when you're with the right person, when you're old enough. Part of the process is gaining the honesty and intimacy to be able to talk to each other about intimate concerns – including contraception. There are lots of books and Web sites that will give you information when you're ready. See page 47 for more help.*

Glossary

bisexual Experiencing sexual attraction to both boys and girls.

blind date A date with someone you have not met before.

body language The nonverbal (not spoken) gestures and expressions that communicate what we are thinking.

contraception Taking precautions during sex to avoid pregnancy.

double date A date that two couples go on at the same time.

emotional Being easily affected by emotions, quick to laugh or cry.

first base (slang) The first step in a relationship – usually kissing.

flirt To behave in a way that is intended to attract another person.

frustration Feeling upset because of your inability to change something.

gay Describes someone who is attracted to people of the same sex.

heterosexual Describes someone who is attracted to people of the opposite sex.

negotiate To try to reach an agreement through discussion.

obsession A persistent idea or emotion that is often unreasonable, and not connected to reality.

possessive Demanding someone's complete attention, not wanting to share him or her with anyone else.

pressurize To put pressure on or force someone to do something that person does not really want to do.

savvy (slang) To be "in the know" or to understand something fully.

socially acceptable What the majority of people think is OK, or how things should be.

stress A physical response to events that makes you feel threatened or upsets your balance. A little stress is good, but a lot of stress can damage your quality of life and your health.

tension A feeling of being under strain, or tense and worried.

tongue-tied Feeling unable to express yourself clearly.

Get help!

There are places to go to if you need more help. The following books and Web sites will give you more information and advice.

Further reading

100 Ways for Every Girl to Look and Feel Fantastic by Alice Hart-Davis (Walker, 2012)

Blame My Brain by Nicola Morgan (Walker, 2007)

Bras, Boys and Bad Hair Days by Anita Naik (Hodder, 2008)

Chicken Soup For The Teenage Soul: Stories of Life, Love and Learning by Jack Canfield and Mark Victor Hansen (Vermilion, 1999)

The Girls' Guide to Guys: Straight Talk for Teens on Flirting, Dating, Breaking Up, Making Up & Finding True Love by Julie Taylor (Three Rivers Press, 2000)

The Rough Guide to Girl Stuff by Kaz Cooke (Rough Guides, 2009)

Teen Love: On Relationships, A Book for Teenagers by Kimberly Kirberger (HCI Teens, 1999)

Web sites

Due to the changing nature of Internet links, Rosen Publishing has developed an online list of Web sites related to the subject of this book. This site is updated regularly. Please use this link to access the list:

http://www.rosenlinks.com/GTALK/Date

Index

A
asking someone out 16, 17, 18, 19, 44

B
bisexual 25
blind dates 5
body language 13
bowling 16, 19, 20, 28, 33
"boy crazy" 9
braces 23
break-ups 8, 29, 36, 37, 43, 44, 45

C
crushes 6, 24, 25

D
dates
  average age 5
  first 20, 21, 28, 29
  friends 10, 11
  ready for 5, 8, 9
double dates 16, 33

F
first base 30, 44
flirting 12

G
gay 25
girlfriends 32, 40
glasses 23

H
health 42, 43
heterosexual 25

K
kissing 7, 8, 22, 23, 30, 38, 39

L
love 6, 10, 11, 17, 19, 24, 25, 27, 29, 32, 45

M
movies 5, 19, 20, 33

P
parents 8, 20, 34, 35, 39
pressure 19, 32, 33

S
saying no 11, 20, 30
sex 25, 30, 31, 45
stress 43